BRADLEY MET

amazon alexa

MORE THAN JUST
WEATHER
& MUSIC

200 WAYS TO USE ALEXA

SCORE PUBLISHING
NASHVILLE, TENNESSEE

First Edition: October 2019

Bradley Metrock serves as CEO of Score Publishing, executive producer of the VoiceFirst Events series (which includes Project Voice, the #1 event for voice tech and AI in America, coming the week after CES), and hosts top tech podcast *This Week In Voice*. For all speaking inquiries, please email info@scorepublishing.us. For information on VoiceFirst Events, visit VoiceFirstEvents.com, and for information specifically on Project Voice, visit ProjectVoice.AI.

Score Publishing, VoiceFirst Events, Project Voice, and *This Week In Voice* are all trademarks of Score Publishing.

Designer/Illustrator: George Otvos
Editor: Lauren Helmer

ISBN 978-0-9911418-9-0

THE RISE OF VOICE

Millions and millions of people, all around the world, are now talking to computers.

They're talking to their smart speakers.
They're talking to their mobile phones.
They're even talking to their appliances.

Children today are growing up with the expectation of being able to speak to technology.

Isn't this the way things were meant to be?

Our mother's voice reverberates in the womb and welcomes us into this world. Soon after, we develop an inner voice, which guides us for the rest of our lives. Didn't it always make sense, then, that technology would arc toward being voice-driven?

The rise of voice doesn't come at the expense of screens. Quite the contrary—screens are now everywhere, even more than we had before.

Yes, privacy issues abound. We need ownership of our data, our experiences, and our voice itself. This new technology will challenge us in new ways.

But the trade-offs will be worth it.

This world didn't always have the QWERTY keyboard and mouse. This world didn't always have smartphones everywhere, dominating our attention. This world did, however, always revolve around the power and simplicity of the human voice.

This is the era we lived in long ago, in times of oral tradition. This is the era we live in now, once again. Voice, first.

For Mason Metrock

Bradley Metrock:
What would a young Mark Cuban be doing with voice technology right now?

Mark Cuban:
I would be writing Alexa skills all day, every day.

This Week In Voice
Season 3 Finale
April 18, 2019

CONTENTS

CONTENTS

CONTENTS

CONTENTS

CONTENTS

FOREWORD

In 1998, Paul Krugman predicted "by 2005 or so, it will become clear that the internet's impact on the economy has been no greater than the fax machine's." He thought the internet's only real use would be allowing people to connect—and that "most people have nothing to say to each other." It's an understatement to say that Krugman was wrong.

The way people experience voice technology today is similar to how they experienced the internet in the '90s. It was exciting, but most people were just using it to visit bookmarked websites and maybe to do a few other basic things. However, some people saw early on that there was a lot more you could do with the internet than visit websites—they used Hotmail's free email, bought books on Amazon, downloaded music with Napster, and blogged on LiveJournal. To echo the title of this book (yes, pun intended!), most people today just use Alexa for basic tasks like asking for the weather forecast and playing music. But some people are getting so much more out of Alexa, and this book will help you do the same.

When I founded VoiceBrew in January 2019 as an email newsletter with tips and advice to help people get the most out of Alexa, I knew one of the biggest challenges Alexa faced was that people weren't really sure what to do with her. Fast-forward eight months—and with great support from this book's author, Bradley Metrock—and tens of thousands of people have signed up to get VoiceBrew's Alexa tips every day. I've been on multiple TV shows and featured in news outlets including *Business Insider*, *Forbes* and *USA Today*. I've learned that, just like the early internet, people want to use Alexa to their full benefit, but they need help learning how.

Smart speakers are one of the most quickly adopted technologies ever. According to Voicebot.ai, more than one in four adults in the US has access to a smart speaker—and that's only five years after Amazon first released the original Echo in 2014. With this kind of adoption, voice is poised to become one of the primary ways that people interact with technology. However, there is one big problem: Most people only use Alexa for an extremely narrow set of tasks. I'm embarrassed to say that before I started VoiceBrew, I mostly used Alexa to play music, get the weather, and set kitchen timers.

There's a simple reason Alexa is so underutilized: People just don't know what to do. And this book will help to change that. *More Than Just Weather & Music* is a richly illustrated guide featuring 200 ways for you to get more out of Alexa. This book is the essential guide that every Alexa user should have.

Just like the internet fundamentally changed the way we do everything—the way we access information, buy things, communicate with people, get ourselves from point A to point B, and so on—voice technology will once again revolutionize our everyday lives. In the not too distant future, your voice will be your main interface with technology. It will be the way you control home appliances, from your shades to your washing machine (and, of course, smart speaker); the way you interact with your car, mobile device, and earbuds; the way you buy things, make dinner plans, and book travel; and, maybe most importantly, the way you access information. Talking is the most natural way people communicate, and it's a wonderful thing that technology is finally catching up. So we can stop tapping, swiping, clicking, and typing and start talking again.

Katherine Prescott
Founder & Editor, VoiceBrew

MORE THAN JUST WEATHER & MUSIC

Inspired by the computer of *Star Trek* lore and buoyed by decades of research and development involving natural language understanding (NLU) and natural language processing (NLP), Amazon released Alexa in the US on June 23, 2015. It wouldn't take long before Alexa devices became a surprise runaway hit, bringing voice-activated technology into homes, offices, cars, hospitals, hotels, schools, and even into our clothing, all across the globe.

Jeff Bezos has demonstrated that Alexa is Amazon's number-one priority. In quarterly earnings statements, the sole quote attributed to Bezos has routinely and exclusively been about Alexa. At the beginning of 2019, Amazon was hiring more people to work on Alexa than Google was hiring across their entire company. They've released numerous pieces of Alexa-enabled hardware, from the Echo, Echo Dot, and Echo Show to Echo Buttons, the Echo Spot, Echo Frames, Echo Loops, and many others. They've encouraged developers, both through promotion as well as monetization, to devote so much precious time and resources to Alexa that there are now over 100,000 apps for Alexa—what the company calls "skills." And now, Alexa dominates popular culture just as much as it dominates industry discussions.

Perhaps it's exactly because of Alexa's meteoric rise that mainstream-use cases for Alexa have lagged behind. According to a study produced by Dashbot, playing music is the number-one use for Alexa, followed closely by asking for weather forecasts. These are the dominant uses of the platform.

So, with 100,000 ways you can use Alexa, we pretty much only use two?

Yep.

But what we're finding out is that when people know about new things their Alexa-enabled devices can do, they try them. And if they like them, they tend to stick around, expanding the horizons of how we're using voice to interact with our smart speakers.

This book provides 200 ways to use Alexa—great skills developed by third-party companies alongside innovative built-in functions you never knew Alexa could do.

And by the time you're done learning about these, you'll be well on your way to getting much more from Alexa than you ever thought possible.

Engage with your phone—send and receive texts, send and receive emails, ring your phone remotely, launch Google Maps navigation, or any number of other apps via voice, and more.

BEST ALEXA SKILLS
(PCMAG.COM)

REQUIRES ONLINE
ACCOUNT

ENABLE: *Alexa, enable Mastermind.*
THEN USE: *Alexa, launch Mastermind.*
Alexa, ask Mastermind to ring my phone.
Alexa, ask Mastermind to text Bob Smith.

Enjoy access to more than 45 different workouts designed to work your core, upper body, lower body, or full body with this best-in-class exercise skill.

17 BEST ALEXA SKILLS FOR HEALTH AND FITNESS (TOM'S GUIDE)

IN-SKILL PURCHASES AVAILABLE

ENHANCED EXPERIENCE WITH SCREENS

ENABLE: *Alexa, enable 7-Minute Workout.*
THEN USE: *Alexa, open 7-Minute Workout.*

Chompers is fun, age-appropriate entertainment for children for the two minutes dentists recommend they brush their teeth. Even better? It tracks streaks of consecutive brushing—they won't want to miss a session.

**ALEXA SKILL OF THE YEAR
(2019 ALEXA CONFERENCE);
2019 CANNES LION**

 ENABLE: *Alexa, enable Chompers.*
THEN USE: *Alexa, launch Chompers.*

Speak a company's name or, if you remember it, its ticker symbol to receive the company's current stock price and the percentage change in price that day.

BEST ALEXA SKILLS
(PCMAG.COM)

ENABLE: *Alexa, enable Opening Bell.*
THEN USE: *Alexa, ask Opening Bell about Southwest Airlines stock. Alexa, ask Opening Bell about CVS.*

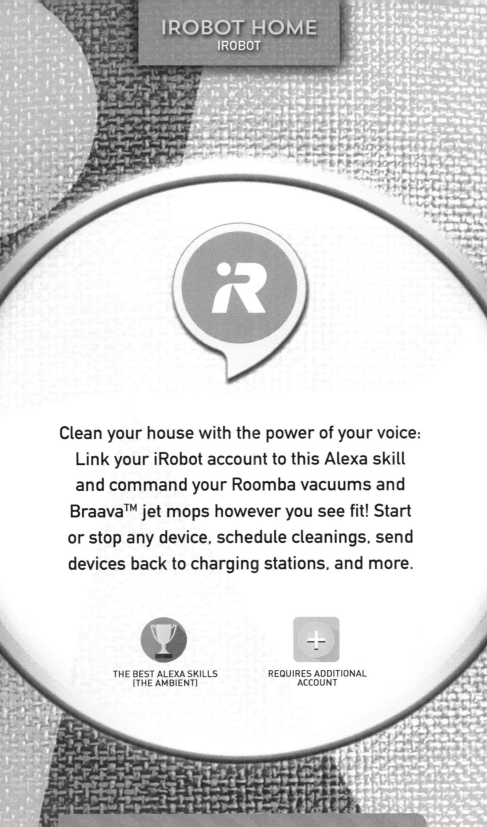

Clean your house with the power of your voice: Link your iRobot account to this Alexa skill and command your Roomba vacuums and Braava™ jet mops however you see fit! Start or stop any device, schedule cleanings, send devices back to charging stations, and more.

THE BEST ALEXA SKILLS
(THE AMBIENT)

REQUIRES ADDITIONAL
ACCOUNT

ENABLE: *Alexa, enable Roomba.*
THEN USE: *Alexa, open Roomba.*
Alexa, ask Roomba to start vacuuming. Alexa, ask Braava to schedule mopping tomorrow night.

DROPPING IN

Alexa-enabled devices allow one user to successfully initiate a voice or video call without requiring the other user to first answer—this feature is called "dropping in." As this is obviously a potentially intrusive feature, all users must go into the Alexa app and identify which specific contacts you will allow to use this feature, if any. And if you do enable the feature but want to temporarily suspend it, go into the Alexa app and enable Do Not Disturb.

Start your day with some positive
inspiration with this highly rated
flash briefing.

FLASH BRIEFING

GREAT FOR
ALL AGES

ENABLE: *Alexa, enable the Everyday Positivity Flash Briefing from the Alexa app or Alexa Skills Store.*

THEN USE: *Alexa, play my flash briefing.*

Use this Alexa skill to learn
about Mars, and get official
updates on the NASA rovers currently
exploring the planet's surface.

GREAT FOR
ALL AGES

ENABLE: *Alexa, enable NASA Mars.*
THEN USE: *Alexa, open NASA Mars.*
Alexa, ask NASA Mars about the Curiosity Rover.

Receive a trivia question each day on topics ranging from literature to science to entertainment. Chain together multiday streaks, unlock extra questions, earn badges with correct answers, and compete against others on leaderboards.

9 POPULAR ALEXA SKILLS TO MAKE YOU SMARTER (CNBC)

IN-SKILL PURCHASES AVAILABLE

ENABLE: *Alexa, enable Question of the Day.*
THEN USE: *Alexa, open Question of the Day.*

This Alexa skill plays the five-minute "Reuters Now" news briefing from the award-winning Reuters global network.

ENHANCED EXPERIENCE
WITH SCREENS

FLASH BRIEFING

ENABLE: *Alexa, enable Reuters TV.*
THEN USE: *Alexa, play my flash briefing.*

Use any Alexa-enabled device to start or stop your Lexus remotely, lock or unlock the doors, check the fuel level, check if your car is running, or check your vehicle's odometer. You can use this skill even if you have multiple Lexus vehicles.

REQUIRES 2015 OR NEWER
LEXUS VEHICLE; ONLINE
ACCOUNT REQUIRED

ENABLE: *Alexa, enable Lexus.*
THEN USE: *Alexa, ask Lexus to start my car.*
Alexa, ask Lexus how much gas is in my car.

THE MAGIC DOOR
THE MAGIC DOOR, LLC

Explore a magical and mysterious
land with this interactive adventure game
for Alexa-enabled devices.

25 AMAZING KID-FRIENDLY
ALEXA SKILLS
(TURBOFUTURE.COM)

ENABLE: *Alexa, enable The Magic Door.*
THEN USE: *Alexa, play The Magic Door.*

This Alexa skill is an excellent companion for a wide variety of chefs. Klove arms you with a library of exclusively curated recipes, which it can then tweak and adjust for you based on your particular preferences. Pair Klove Chef with its mobile app to track cooking times.

ADDITIONAL ACCOUNT
SUGGESTED

ENABLE: *Alexa, enable Klove Chef.*
THEN USE: *Alexa, open Klove Chef.*
Alexa, ask Klove Chef to give me a recipe.

MAKE A DONATION

You can say "Alexa, make a donation," and Alexa will ask you for a charity name and a dollar amount, then use your Amazon account payment information to complete the transaction. Alternatively, if you already know you want to contribute $50 to the United Way, you can specify these things up front: "Alexa, donate $50 to the United Way."

Find the cheapest gas and get
real-time ratings on nearby gas stations
and convenience stores.

REQUIRES ADDITIONAL
ACCOUNT

ENABLE: *Alexa, enable GasBuddy.*
THEN USE: *Alexa, launch GasBuddy.*
Alexa, ask GasBuddy to find the cheapest gas.

Diagnose your pet's illness with Alexa
at no cost, and if necessary, speak live with
a US-licensed veterinarian, available
24 hours a day, for an additional fee.

**FEE TO SPEAK LIVE WITH
VETERINARIANS**

ENABLE: *Alexa, enable MyPetDoc.*
THEN USE: *Alexa, launch MyPetDoc.*
Alexa, tell MyPetDoc my dog has fleas.

Solve the mystery of who killed Bruce Wayne's parents. *The Wayne Investigation* has been so successful, it caused Amazon to begin funding other developers to create Alexa-based games.

**THE BEST GAMES
TO PLAY WITH ALEXA
[DIGITAL TRENDS]**

**PARENTAL GUIDANCE
SUGGESTED**

ENABLE: *Alexa, enable The Wayne Investigation.*
THEN USE: *Alexa, launch The Wayne Investigation.*

Keep track of a variety of statistics related
to your new, or even unborn, child
with this Alexa skill. Track everything
from the baby's in-utero kicks and feedings
to sleep time and stool-and-urine tracking.

ONE OF THE BEST
ALEXA SKILLS FOR MOMS
[MASHABLE]

ADDITIONAL ACCOUNT
RECOMMENDED

ENABLE: *Alexa, enable Baby Stats.*
THEN USE: *Alexa, ask Baby Stats how many*
feedings in the last 24 hours. Alexa, ask Baby Stats
to add feeding 3 ounces with the right breast.

Use your Alexa-enabled smart speaker or device to tune your guitar, as it plays notes starting from low E to high E.

THE BEST ALEXA SKILLS
(THE AMBIENT)

ENABLE: *Alexa, enable Guitar Tuner.*
THEN USE: *Alexa, open Guitar Tuner.*
Alexa, ask Guitar Tuner to tune my guitar.

Speak to Alexa to place your usual Starbucks
order at one of your recently visited
locations, so it's ready for you upon arrival.
With this Alexa skill, you can also check
a Starbucks gift card balance.

THE BEST ALEXA SKILLS
(THE AMBIENT)

REQUIRES ONLINE
ACCOUNT

ENHANCED EXPERIENCE
WITH SCREENS

ENABLE: *Alexa, enable Starbucks.*
THEN USE: *Alexa, open Starbucks.*
Alexa, ask Starbucks to start my usual order.

StatMuse is the sports fan's dream, allowing you to hear about all manner of sports statistics from players and sports personalities themselves.

GREAT FOR
ALL AGES

ENABLE: *Alexa, enable StatMuse.*
THEN USE: *Alexa, open StatMuse. Alexa, ask StatMuse which quarterback had the best year last year.*

HOW YOU REMIND ME

Need help remembering to give your pet his meds every 12 weeks or remembering to change that forgettable fridge filter every six months? Or maybe it's your one turn to bring snacks to the soccer game? At any date and time you choose, whether it's a one-time thing or a regular occurrence, Alexa can give you personal reminders. Go to the Alexa app, go to Reminders & Alarms in the main menu, and navigate to Reminders to get started.

Ask Alexa to play music and audiobooks
you've borrowed from your local
public library, courtesy
of Hoopla Digital's Alexa skill.

**REQUIRES
ADDITIONAL ACCOUNT**

**GREAT FOR
ALL AGES**

ENABLE: *Alexa, enable Hoopla Digital.*
THEN USE: *Alexa, open Hoopla Digital.*
Alexa, ask Hoopla Digital to list my audiobooks.

Ask Alexa to translate short phrases
or sentences from English into one
of 37 major languages.

BEST ALEXA SKILLS
(PCMAG.COM)

ENABLE: *Alexa, enable Translated.*
THEN USE: *Alexa, open Translated.*
Alexa, say "Is it raining today?" in Italian.
Alexa, say "time to say goodbye" in Spanish.

Kids having a squabble? Open Kids Court and let Judge Lexy give the final verdict. You can also play the judge in the fights of other kids, with new trials being added daily.

WON 2018 ALEXA SKILLS CHALLENGE

IN-SKILL PURCHASES AVAILABLE

ENHANCED EXPERIENCE WITH SCREENS

ENABLE: *Alexa, enable Kids Court.*
THEN USE: *Alexa, open Kids Court.*
Alexa, be a judge in Kids Court.

MARKETPLACE
MAKE
ME SMART

Listen to the popular "Make Me Smart
with Kai and Molly" podcast with this Alexa
skill, and learn something new each day about
economics, technology, and culture.

9 POPULAR ALEXA
SKILLS THAT WILL MAKE
YOU SMARTER
(CNBC)

ENABLE: *Alexa, enable Make Me Smart.*
THEN USE: *Alexa, open Make Me Smart.*

Send money, receive money, and check your
PayPal balance all with the power of your
voice. It's easiest to use the PayPal skill
to interact with your saved contacts,
so make sure that list is updated.

**REQUIRES ADDITIONAL
ACCOUNT**

ENABLE: *Alexa, enable PayPal.*
THEN USE: *Alexa, send $100 to Ray. Alexa,
request $200 from Jody. Alexa, open PayPal
and check my balance.*

Discover new Twitch broadcasters
and play Twitch channels using the official
Twitch skill for Alexa-enabled devices.

**PARENTAL GUIDANCE
SUGGESTED**

**ENHANCED EXPERIENCE
WITH SCREENS**

**REQUIRES ADDITIONAL
ACCOUNT**

ENABLE: *Alexa, enable Twitch.*
THEN USE: *Alexa, play Twitch.*

With this Expedia skill, you can ask Alexa
about travel destinations and whether
they fit your particular interests and budget.

THE 12 MOST USEFUL SKILLS
FOR PLANNING A VACATION
(TRIPSAVVY.COM)

ENABLE: *Alexa, enable Expedia.*
THEN USE: *Alexa, open Expedia. Alexa,
ask Expedia to tell me about popular
attractions in London.*

SHOW AND TELL

Take any product, hold it up to the camera
of any Echo Show, and ask, "Alexa, what am
I holding?" And Alexa will tell you about the product.
This feature, which was created with accessibility
in mind, is useful for vision-impaired
and memory-impaired people.

The Earplay skill features an assortment
of award-winning interactive stories
and narrative experiences produced
with stellar voice acting and sound effects.
Get lost in a new world for a while.

BEST ALEXA SKILLS
(PCMAG.COM)

PG

PARENTAL GUIDANCE
SUGGESTED

ENABLE: *Alexa, enable Earplay.*
THEN USE: *Alexa, open Earplay.*

Record migraines and their length
with this Alexa skill, and view
the data anywhere within
Migraine Buddy's companion app.

ENABLE: *Alexa, enable Migraine Buddy.*
THEN USE: *Alexa, open Migraine Buddy.*
Alexa, ask Migraine Buddy to record a migraine.

Get ideas for specific activities that fathers can do with their children, based on the book *Daddy Saturday: How To Be An Intentional Dad to Raise Good Kids Who Become Great Adults.*

ENABLE: *Alexa, enable Daddy Saturday.*
THEN USE: *Alexa, play Daddy Saturday.*
Alexa, ask Daddy Saturday what to do this Thursday.

This skill, from Procter & Gamble, will help walk you through step-by-step instructions for your laundry routine so you can remove even the toughest stains. With help from Alexa, answer up to 200 questions involving the most stubborn stains.

ENABLE: *Alexa, enable Tide.*
THEN USE: *Alexa, open Tide.*
Alexa ask Tide how I should wash silk?
Alexa, ask Tide how do I remove a chocolate stain?

Sing along to a wide variety of children's songs, either with vocals or as instrumental versions, with this fun karaoke skill.

3 ALEXA SKILLS YOU NEED TO KNOW RIGHT NOW (KIM KOMANDO)

GREAT FOR ALL AGES

 ENABLE: *Alexa, enable Kids Karaoke.*
THEN USE: *Alexa, play Kids Karaoke.*

With The Bartender, Alexa can
now tell you how to make
thousands of alcoholic drinks.

PG

PARENTAL GUIDANCE
SUGGESTED

ENAHNCED EXPERIENCE
WITH SCREENS

ENABLE: *Alexa, enable The Bartender.*
THEN USE: *Alexa, launch The Bartender.*
Alexa, ask The Bartender to make me a margarita.

Sync to your Any.do account and add
or change tasks to your to-do list or shopping
list through Alexa. These lists will then be
accessible on any device.

REQUIRES ADDITIONAL
ACCOUNT

ENABLE: *Alexa, enable Any.do.*
THEN USE: *Alexa, add paper towels to my
shopping list. Alexa, add reading More Than
Just Weather & Music to my to-do list.*

GETTING
INTO ROUTINES

You can have Alexa initiate multiple functions
with one single verbal command using
Alexa Routines. From the Alexa app menu options,
navigate to Routines. Select the plus sign
to begin creating a new Routine, where you
can give Alexa instructions on what
input to receive and, upon receipt, what
output to deliver and in what sequence.

storytime

With this skill, Amazon provides a library of over 100 professionally narrated short stories primarily aimed at children ages 5-12.

19 GREAT ALEXA SKILLS FOR KIDS AND TEENS (COMMON SENSE MEDIA)

IN-SKILL PURCHASES AVAILABLE

GREAT FOR ALL AGES

ENABLE: *Alexa, enable Amazon Storytime.*
THEN USE: *Alexa, play Amazon Storytime. Alexa, ask Amazon Storytime to tell me a LEGO story. Alexa, ask Amazon Storytime to tell me a Ripley's Believe It Or Not! story.*

Stay up to date on hurricanes affecting
your area with this Alexa skill from
the American Red Cross. Activate push
notifications to receive real-time alerts,
and hear information on how to stay safe
should you find yourself in a storm zone.

**8 BEST NEW ALEXA
SKILLS & UPDATES
(VOICEBREW)**

ENABLE: *Alexa, enable Hurricane Alerts.*
THEN USE: *Alexa, open Hurricane Alerts.*

Dietitian Ashley Koff provides a wealth of health knowledge with her Alexa skill. You can ask one of over 200 nutrition-related questions, request a daily health tip, or get a pep talk to nudge you toward healthier—and just as delicious—food, drinks, and even recipes.

**8 BEST NEW ALEXA
SKILLS & UPDATES
(VOICEBREW)**

ENABLE: *Alexa, enable My Better Nutrition.*
THEN USE: *Alexa, open My Better Nutrition.*

Get started with Clever Real Estate,
a company that will list most houses for
a flat fee of $3,000 while using highly rated,
licensed realtors. Save money and get
top-notch service by using this Alexa skill.

ENABLE: *Alexa, enable Clever Real Estate.*
THEN USE: *Alexa, open Clever Real Estate.*

With the AnyPod Alexa skill, you can listen
to thousands of popular podcasts on topics
ranging from culture to technology
to comedy to business and more.

TOP ALEXA SKILL OF 2018
(DIGITAL TRENDS)

ENABLE: *Alexa, enable AnyPod.*
THEN USE: *Alexa, open AnyPod.*
Alexa, ask AnyPod to play The Daily.

Alexa can play any number of relaxing sounds
to lull you to sleep, from thunderstorms
to rain to oceans and more.

ONE OF THE FIRST 7 SKILLS
YOU SHOULD ENABLE
(CNET)

IN-SKILL PURCHASES
AVAILABLE

GREAT FOR
ALL AGES

ENABLE: *Alexa, enable Sleep Sounds.*
THEN USE: *Alexa, play Sleep Sounds.*
Alexa, ask Sleep Sounds for rain.

From the editors of *The Economist*,
this Alexa skill can tell you about events
in business and politics from the last
24 hours, the top five recent articles,
or a quote of the day.

AMAZON ECHO
TIPS AND TRICKS
(DIGITAL TRENDS)

ENABLE: *Alexa, enable Espresso.*
THEN USE: *Alexa, open Espresso.*
Alexa, ask Espresso for the World in Brief.

SAVE
THE DATE

You can link your calendar to Alexa, making
it easy to verbally add an event to your schedule
or have Alexa remind you of your upcoming
meetings. Go to the Alexa app, go to the menu
and navigate to Settings, select Calendar & Email,
and choose which type of calendar you'd like.

Order a car to pick you up at anytime,
day or night, just by asking Alexa.
Ask about your ride's status, rate
your driver, and more.

BEST ALEXA SKILLS
(PCMAG.COM)

REQUIRES ADDITIONAL
ACCOUNT

ENABLE: *Alexa, enable Lyft.*
THEN USE: *Alexa, open Lyft.*
Alexa, ask Lyft to take me to work.

The History Channel's Alexa skill
will tell you historical facts from the current
day or from any day of your choice.

2018 WEBBY AWARD

GREAT FOR
ALL AGES

ENABLE: *Alexa, enable This Day In History.*
THEN USE: *Alexa, launch This Day In History. Alexa, ask This Day In History what happened on September 22.*

Use this Alexa skill to get real-time updates on your fantasy football roster, as well as an overview of your team's matchup and opponent. Alexa-enabled devices with screens will have access to a weekly video forecasting your team's projected performance.

ENHANCED EXPERIENCE WITH SCREENS

REQUIRES ADDITIONAL ACCOUNT

This Alexa skill—best used on Alexa devices
with screens, such as the Echo Show—provides
fun, easy tutorials on how to chop
all kinds of fresh produce.

**THE 22 BEST USES
FOR ALEXA TODAY
(VOICEBREW)**

**ENHANCED EXPERIENCE
WITH SCREENS**

ENABLE: *Alexa, enable Chop Chop.*
THEN USE: *Alexa, open Chop Chop.*

Access Comcast Business features through any Alexa-enabled device, notably including the ability to initiate or join an audio conference call without having to know phone numbers, IDs, or pin numbers.

REQUIRES ADDITIONAL ACCOUNT

ENABLE: *Alexa, enable Comcast Business.*
THEN USE: *Alexa, open Comcast Business.*
Alexa, ask Comcast Business to start a conference on my mobile.

Children can use this fun holiday Alexa skill
to add items to their wish list or to report
their good behavior to Saint Nick himself.
Even better: When your child tells Santa
something they want for Christmas,
the owner of the Amazon account receives
an email with the gift request.

**GREAT FOR
ALL AGES**

ENABLE: *Alexa, enable Dear Santa.*
THEN USE: *Alexa, open Dear Santa.*

Get first-aid information from
the healthcare leaders at Mayo Clinic
for dozens of common health
problems or first-aid situations.

ALEXA HEALTHCARE
SKILL OF THE YEAR
(2019 ALEXA CONFERENCE)

ENABLE: *Alexa, enable Mayo Clinic First Aid.*
THEN USE: *Alexa, launch Mayo Clinic First Aid.*
Alexa, ask Mayo Clinic First Aid about chest pain.

SPEAKING IN YOUR OWN VOICE

Alexa has the ability to recognize individual voices, which can allow Alexa to identify particular users within a family or household and select their own music, when prompted, or make calls to particular contacts based on who is asking to make the call. To personalize your experience and allow Alexa to identify you by your voice, go to the Alexa app, go to Settings, go to Alexa Account, go to Recognized Voices, and enable this feature.

Alert your family and close network that you need help. Or let them know you're OK with this skill's "check in" feature.

WON 2018 AARP PURPOSE PRIZE

IN-SKILL PURCHASES AVAILABLE

REQUIRES ONLINE ACCOUNT

ENABLE: *Alexa, enable Ask My Buddy.*
THEN USE: *Alexa, Ask My Buddy to send help.*
Alexa, Ask My Buddy to check in with mom.

Play a fun, family-friendly game in which various players take turns choosing between two silly, lighthearted scenarios.

**THE BEST GAMES
TO PLAY WITH ALEXA
[DIGITAL TRENDS]**

**IN-SKILL PURCHASES
AVAILABLE**

**GREAT FOR
ALL AGES**

ENABLE: *Alexa, enable Would You Rather.*
THEN USE: *Alexa, play Would You Rather.*

SIMPLISAFE HOME CONTROL
SIMPLISAFE

Enable your SimpliSafe home security system, and conveniently put it into home or away mode, using SimpliSafe's Alexa skill.

ENABLE: *Alexa, enable SimpliSafe.*
THEN USE: *Alexa, open SimpliSafe. Alexa, ask SimpliSafe to arm my system in away mode.*

This throwback Alexa skill
plays vintage radio dramas
from CBS Radio Mystery Theater.

ENABLE: *Alexa, enable Radio Mystery Theater.*
THEN USE: *Alexa, open Radio Mystery Theater.*

Provide information and services to guests staying at your rental properties with this best-in-class Alexa skill.

2018 VRMA INNOVATOR OF THE YEAR

REQUIRES ADDITIONAL ACCOUNT

ENABLE: *Alexa, enable Virtual Concierge Service.*
THEN USE: *Alexa, open Virtual Concierge Service.*

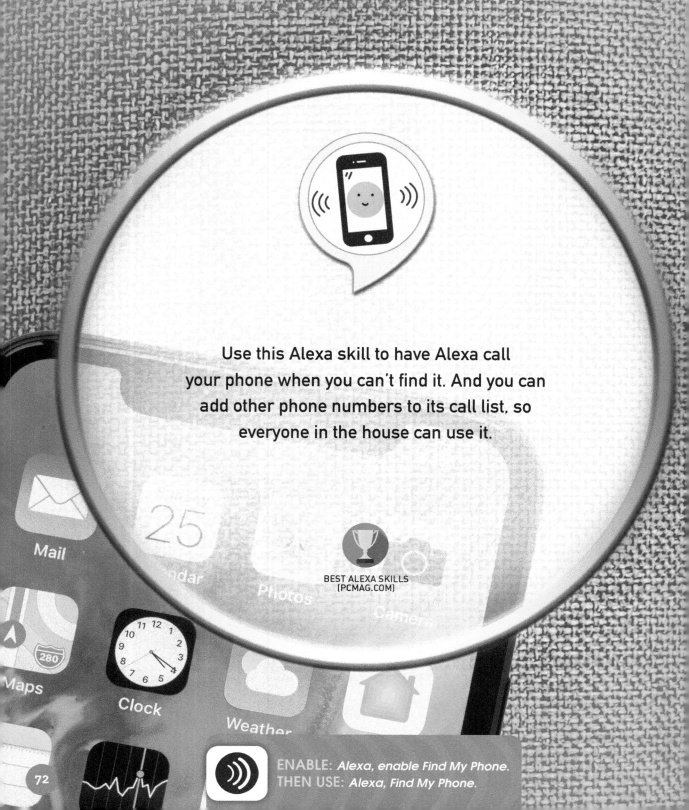

Use this Alexa skill to have Alexa call your phone when you can't find it. And you can add other phone numbers to its call list, so everyone in the house can use it.

BEST ALEXA SKILLS
(PCMAG.COM)

ENABLE: *Alexa, enable Find My Phone.*
THEN USE: *Alexa, Find My Phone.*

STOP SMOKING COACH
CALIFORNIA SMOKERS HELPLINE
AT UC SAN DIEGO

Get tips on how to quit smoking,
or sign up to speak with a coach
from the California Smokers Helpline
who can help you quit.

ENABLE: *Alexa, enable Stop Smoking Coach.*
THEN USE: *Alexa, open Stop Smoking Coach.*

FOLLOW-UP MODE

In an effort to make Alexa more conversational, Follow-up Mode allows you to ask Alexa a sequence of questions without repeating the wake word each time. Go to the Alexa app, go to the Devices tab, select a device, and navigate to Follow-up Mode to toggle this mode on or off.

This is beautiful footage of a live aquarium,
set to soothing music, designed primarily
for use with Echo devices with screens,
such as the Echo Show.

ENHANCED EXPERIENCE
WITH SCREENS

ENABLE: *Alexa, enable Fish Tank.*
THEN USE: *Alexa, play Fish Tank.*

This Alexa skill provides a new suggested
act of kindness each day, from a library
of more than 50 acts of kindness to share with
family, friends, and maybe even a stranger.

**GREAT FOR
ALL AGES**

ENABLE: *Alexa, enable Daily Kindness.*
THEN USE: *Alexa, open Daily Kindness.*

When you see a business that features the Send Me a Sample logo, simply say "Alexa, send me a sample" and you'll receive a free product sample from that business in the mail.

REQUIRES ADDITIONAL ACCOUNT

ENABLE: *Alexa, enable Send Me a Sample.*
THEN USE: *Alexa, open Send Me a Sample.*

Intended for children, this skill allows kids to experience daily stories that center around exploration.

GREAT FOR ALL AGES

ENABLE: *Alexa, enable Daily Adventure.*
THEN USE: *Alexa, open Daily Adventure.*

ELLE
HOROSCOPES
BY THE ASTROTWINS

Get your daily horoscope from
The Astro Twins, the identical twin sisters best
known as the "astrologists for the stars."

BEST ALEXA SKILLS OF 2018
(BEST PRODUCTS)

ENABLE: *Alexa, enable Horoscope.*
THEN USE: *Alexa, open Horoscope.*
Alexa, ask Horoscope for the horoscope for Virgo.

Track claim information and get personalized weekly updates on SmartRide, Nationwide's discount driving program that rewards safe drivers.

ENABLE: *Alexa, enable Nationwide.*
THEN USE: *Alexa, open Nationwide.*
Alexa, ask Nationwide about my SmartRide status.

Players must answer questions previously
posed to groups of 100 people, trying
to guess the least popular responses
in order to gain the fewest possible points.
The player with the least points wins.

BEST ALEXA TRIVIA SKILLS
(TOM'S GUIDE)

IN-SKILL PURCHASES
AVAILABLE

ENABLE: *Alexa, enable Pointless.*
THEN USE: *Alexa, play Pointless.*

PHONE
A FRIEND
(EITHER PHONE OR SKYPE)

Alexa can make or receive audio or video calls.
For people in your contact list, you can say
"Alexa, call John Smith," and Alexa will initiate the call.
You can also initiate audio or video calls out of the Alexa app
itself. You can even use Skype with Alexa to place
and receive calls—go to the Alexa app, navigate to
Settings within the menu options,
select Skype, and sign in.

Enjoy the massive collection of TED Talks, which can be listened to by topic or speaker, or you can have Alexa randomly select one for you. The skill is updated weekly with new talks, so you can always find new topics and perspectives to expand your horizons.

BEST ALEXA SKILLS
(PCMAG.COM)

ENABLE: *Alexa, enable TED Talks.*
THEN USE: *Alexa, open TED Talks.*
Alexa, ask TED Talks for a talk about space.

This official skill of Ubisoft's video game "Assassin's Creed: Odyssey" allows users to engage with Alexios, one of the game's main characters. Ask him anything you might normally ask Alexa—What's the weather?—or ask questions related to in-game characters, settings, or plot points for more detailed information.

PG

PARENTAL GUIDANCE
SUGGESTED

ENABLE: *Alexa, enable The Spartan.*
THEN USE: *Alexa, open The Spartan. Alexa, ask The Spartan to tell me about the Athenian Treasury.*

Get information on store locations, hours, in-store events, return policies, and more with Macy's official Alexa skill.

ENABLE: *Alexa, enable Macy's.*
THEN USE: *Alexa, open Macy's. Alexa, ask Macy's about the return policy. Alexa, ask Macy's about the Star Rewards program.*

TuneIn Live allows you to access thousands of live sporting events, premium news stations, and sports talk radio stations from any Alexa-enabled device.

FEE TO SIGN UP FOR TUNEIN LIVE ACCOUNT

ENABLE: *Alexa, enable TuneIn Live.*
THEN USE: *Alexa, open TuneIn Live.*
Alexa, ask TuneIn Live to play MSNBC.

Enjoy this fun, Sudoku-like puzzle game
in which an evil villain hides your
special blob in one of 12 universes,
and you must try to save it.

GREAT FOR
ALL AGES

ENABLE: *Alexa, enable Save the Blob.*
THEN USE: *Alexa, open Save the Blob.*

Receive a new daily guided meditation
through Alexa, as well as access
to a sleep exercise designed to help
you relax at the end of a busy day.

9 POPULAR ALEXA
SKILLS THAT WILL
MAKE YOU SMARTER
(CNBC)

ADDITIONAL ACCOUNT
REQUIRED

ENABLE: *Alexa, play Headspace.*
THEN USE: *Alexa, open Headspace.*
Alexa, tell Headspace I'm ready for bed.

STEPHEN KING

Answer a series of questions and this Alexa skill will produce a customized list of Stephen King books you should read, from among the 50+ he's written.

DIGITAL BOOK WORLD
2018 ALEXA SKILL
OF THE YEAR

ENABLE: *Alexa, enable Stephen King Library.*
THEN USE: *Alexa, open Stephen King Library.*
Alexa, ask Stephen King Library for my last reading list.

MAKING ANNOUNCEMENTS

Whether you're trying to reach people at home and they're not picking up the phone, or whether you want to broadcast throughout your house that dinner is ready, you can make Announcements through Alexa-enabled devices. Open the Alexa app, navigate to Communicate within the bottom navigation bar, touch the Announce button, and input your message.

With this official skill from UPS, you can conveniently track your packages, find the nearest UPS Store, or get a shipping quote without having to leave your home.

UPS MY CHOICE ACCOUNT
REQUIRED FOR MOST
FUNCTIONS

ENABLE: *Alexa, enable UPS.*
THEN USE: *Alexa, open UPS. Alexa, ask UPS if I have packages arriving today. Alexa, find the closest UPS store.*

You are trapped in a room. Figure out how to escape by searching your environment, picking up items, and solving puzzles.

**THE BEST GAMES
TO PLAY WITH ALEXA
[DIGITAL TRENDS]**

**IN-SKILL PURCHASES
AVAILABLE**

ENABLE: *Alexa, enable Escape the Room.*
THEN USE: *Alexa, play Escape the Room.*

ZYRTEC
YOUR DAILY ALLERGYCAST
JOHNSON & JOHNSON

Receive a daily allergy report containing weather information, pollen count, and local allergens within your area. Zyrtec's Alexa skill will then compute an "Allergy Impact" score, quantifying how the allergens in your area may affect you during the day.

TOP 7 HEALTH CARE ALEXA SKILLS
(VOICEMARKETDATA)

ENABLE: *Alexa, enable Zyrtec.*
THEN USE: *Alexa, open Zyrtec.*
Alexa, ask Zyrtec for my AllergyCast.

Participate in periodic, exclusive
Reebok sneaker drops available
only through this Alexa skill.

ENABLE: *Alexa, enable Reebok Sneaker Drop.*
THEN USE: *Alexa, open Reebok Sneaker Drop.*

Enjoy the classic word game:
Provide words as prompted to create
your own hilarious and silly story!

ONE OF THE BEST ALEXA
SKILLS FOR KIDS AND
PARENTS 2018
(MASHABLE)

GREAT FOR
ALL AGES

ENABLE: *Alexa, enable Mad Libs.*
THEN USE: *Alexa, open Mad Libs.*
Alexa, ask Mad Libs for a new story.

Test your child's arithmetic ability in addition, subtraction, multiplication, and division through a mix of numerical and word problems across five difficulty levels.

BEST MULTI-MODAL EXPERIENCE
(2019 VOICE SUMMIT)

ENHANCED EXPERIENCE WITH SCREENS

ONLINE PARENTAL ACCOUNT AVAILABLE

ENABLE: *Alexa, enable Bamboo Math.*
THEN USE: *Alexa, launch Bamboo Math.*

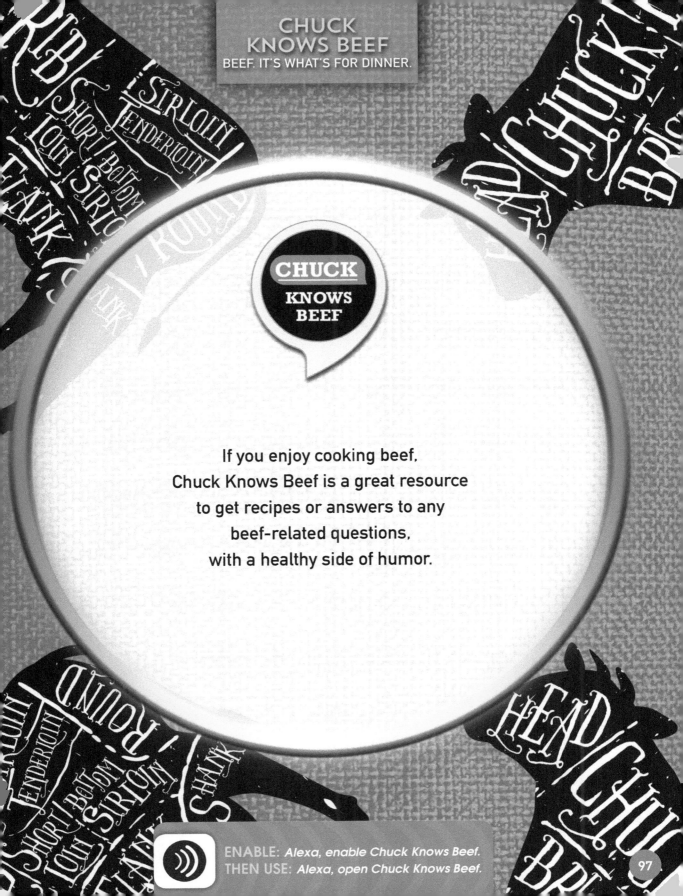

CHUCK
KNOWS
BEEF

If you enjoy cooking beef,
Chuck Knows Beef is a great resource
to get recipes or answers to any
beef-related questions,
with a healthy side of humor.

ENABLE: *Alexa, enable Chuck Knows Beef.*
THEN USE: *Alexa, open Chuck Knows Beef.*

THE
RIGHT STUFF

Ask, "Alexa, where's my stuff?" to get
a real-time summary of where
your Amazon packages are
in the delivery process.

This is a fun Alexa skill that, upon command,
plays sound similar to *Star Trek*'s "red alert"
audio. It's perfect for linking up with
smart-home routines or simply surprising
the science fiction fan in the house.

ENABLE: *Alexa, enable Red Alert.*
THEN USE: *Alexa, Red Alert!*

CALM MY DOG
HERO SOFTWARE

Play slow-tempo classical music specifically chosen to calm your dog. A premium upgrade provides better sound quality and longer audio loops to keep your pet company while you're away.

IN-SKILL PURCHASES AVAILABLE

ENABLE: *Alexa, enable Calm My Dog.*
THEN USE: *Alexa, open Calm My Dog.*

This Alexa skill allows you to control a wide variety of Dyson-connected machines with your voice. Fans, heaters, purifiers, robots, and more can all provide information and receive commands to make your life a little easier.

REQUIRES ONLINE ACCOUNT

ENABLE: *Alexa, enable Dyson.*
THEN USE: *Alexa, open Dyson.*

Play Heads Up! on Alexa and enjoy the same guessing game that Ellen plays with guests on her show. A variety of questions come free with the skill, and more are available to purchase if desired.

THE BEST GAMES TO PLAY WITH ALEXA (DIGITAL TRENDS)

IN-SKILL PURCHASES AVAILABLE

PARENTAL GUIDANCE SUGGESTED (FOR ADULTS-ONLY EXPANSION)

ENABLE: *Alexa, enable Heads Up!*
THEN USE: *Alexa, open Heads Up!*

This Alexa skill will read aloud
one of several short bedtime stories,
personalized with the name of your
child or whomever you choose.

**25 AMAZING KID-FRIENDLY
ALEXA SKILLS
(TURBOFUTURE.COM)**

**GREAT FOR
ALL AGES**

ENABLE: *Alexa, enable Bedtime Story.*
THEN USE: *Alexa, open Bedtime Story.*
Alexa, tell Bedtime Story to Mason.

Challenge Alexa in this game made famous by the TV show *The Big Bang Theory*. Enjoy global and city-based leaderboards viewable through any Echo device with a screen.

ENHANCED EXPERIENCE WITH SCREENS

IN-SKILL PURCHASES AVAILABLE

GREAT FOR ALL AGES

ENABLE: *Alexa, enable Lizard Spock.*
THEN USE: *Alexa, play Lizard Spock.*

ring

Manage all of your Ring devices, from your alarm to your locks to your cameras and more, with this Alexa skill. Get video from your cameras on Alexa-enabled devices with screens, or simply speak to your home security system through Alexa on any device.

THE BEST ALEXA SKILLS
(THE AMBIENT)

ENHANCED EXPERIENCE
WITH SCREENS

REQUIRES ADDITIONAL
ACCOUNT

ENABLE: *Alexa, enable Ring.*
THEN USE: *Alexa, open Ring.*
Alexa, arm Ring.

ALEXA
MEASURES UP

When you're cooking in one of any number
of hands-free situations, Alexa can help
you convert one measurement to another with ease.
Ask "Alexa, how many cups are in a quart?" or "Alexa,
how many centimeters are in a foot?"

Enjoy daily updates and, with a paid in-skill subscription, live play-by-play commentary from the English Premier League.

IN-SKILL PURCHASES AVAILABLE

ENABLE: *Alexa, enable Premier League Live.*
THEN USE: *Alexa, open Premier League Live. Alexa, ask Premier League Live to play the Manchester United game.*

Talk to Me

Talk To Me, a book published by Houghton Mifflin Harcourt by journalist and entrepreneur James Vlahos, chronicles the rise of voice computing to becoming an integral part of modern society. This Alexa skill will have the author read you a passage from the book, share a brief summary of the book in his own words, or lead you in a game based on the book.

ENABLE: *Alexa, enable The Voice Computing Book.*
THEN USE: *Alexa, open The Voice Computing Book.*

Chart your own course in these classic
Choose Your Own Adventure stories,
each professionally narrated and featuring
a wide variety of potential outcomes.

8 BEST NEW ALEXA
SKILLS & UPDATES
(VOICEBREW)

ENABLE: *Alexa, enable Choose Your Own Adventure.*
THEN USE: *Alexa, open Choose Your Own Adventure.*

Use NPR on Alexa to play NPR
or listen to a specific city's NPR station.

BEST ALEXA SKILLS
(PCMAG.COM)

ENABLE: *Alexa, enable NPR.*
THEN USE: *Alexa, play NPR. Alexa,*
ask NPR to play WPLN.

The Adobe XD skill allows developers using Adobe XD to interact with and preview voice-driven prototypes through Alexa-enabled devices.

REQUIRES ADDITIONAL ACCOUNT

ENABLE: *Navigate to Adobe XD within Amazon's Alexa Skills Marketplace to enable.*
THEN USE: *Alexa, open Adobe XD.*

With Valossa Movie Finder, you can search from one of the world's largest databases of films by saying what a movie is about, and this Alexa skill will return a list of top results.

PG

PARENTAL GUIDANCE
SUGGESTED

ENABLE: *Alexa, enable Valossa Movie Finder.*
THEN USE: *Alexa, open Valossa Movie Finder.*

Better prepare for standardized tests, or simply get smarter, by using this Alexa skill. SAT Word of the Day includes spelling, definition, and sample sentences for each day's word.

GREAT FOR
ALL AGES

ENABLE: *Alexa, enable SAT Word of the Day.*
THEN USE: *Alexa, open SAT Word of the Day. Alexa, ask SAT Word of the Day for the word of the day.*

LET THERE BE LIGHT

Alexa is compatible with a wide array
of smart lighting systems, from Philips Hue
to Samsung SmartThings to LIFX smart bulbs
to Wyze bulbs and several others. All have Alexa
skills that can be enabled from the Alexa Skills Store
and linked to your hardware's online account.

100%
Gluten Free
News

This Alexa skill is a flash briefing
that curates news, products, and events to
help you and your family live a gluten-free life.

FLASH BRIEFING

ENABLE: *Alexa, enable Gluten Free News.*
THEN USE: *Alexa, play my flash briefing.*

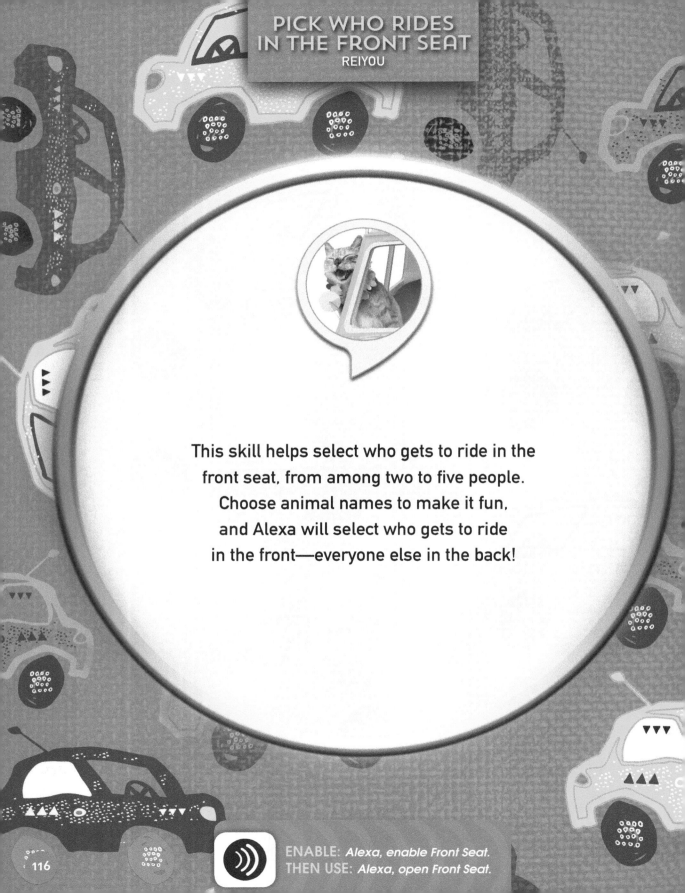

This skill helps select who gets to ride in the
front seat, from among two to five people.
Choose animal names to make it fun,
and Alexa will select who gets to ride
in the front—everyone else in the back!

ENABLE: *Alexa, enable Front Seat.*
THEN USE: *Alexa, open Front Seat.*

Jeopardy! lets you test your knowledge
on a new set of questions every single day,
from pop culture and travel to world history
and technology, as well as Teen Jeopardy!
and Sports Jeopardy! on Sundays.

BEST ALEXA SKILLS
(PCMAG.COM)

TECHNOLOGY

THE GREAT
OUTDOORS

SPEAK OF
THE DICKENS

$200 $200 $200 $200

$400 $400 $400 $400 $400 $400

$600

ENABLE: *Alexa, enable Jeopardy!*
THEN USE: *Alexa, play Jeopardy!*

HOLY BIBLE

Choose from five different
professionally narrated Bible versions,
and read verses or receive a verse
of the day. Link a YouVersion account
and listen to daily reading plans.

+

ADDITIONAL ACCOUNT
RECOMMENDED

ENABLE: *Alexa, enable YouVerson Bible.*
THEN USE: *Alexa, open YouVersion Bible.*
Alexa, ask YouVersion Bible to read John 3:16.

This simple Alexa skill activates Alexa's blue light for five minutes, helping you see in a darkened room, or helping you locate a light switch or buttons on an Echo device.

ENABLE: *Alexa, enable Sleep Light.*
THEN USE: *Alexa, open Sleep Light.*

Beat the Intro is the ultimate music game for Alexa-enabled devices. Guess a song's title and artist as quickly as possible to gain points. Compete online against the world or locally against friends and family.

THE BEST GAMES TO PLAY WITH ALEXA [DIGITAL TRENDS]

IN-SKILL PURCHASES AVAILABLE

ENHANCED EXPERIENCE WITH SCREENS

ENABLE: *Alexa, enable Beat the Intro.*
THEN USE: *Alexa, play Beat the Intro.*

Learn all about the keto diet—what to eat, what to avoid, and the various benefits of adhering to a ketogenic diet.

ENABLE: *Alexa, enable Keto Guide.*
THEN USE: *Alexa, open Keto Guide.*

SHOPPING WITH ALEXA

Want to order an item? Say "Alexa, order toothbrushes." Alexa will take data from your order history, along with information on highest-reviewed products in that category, to fulfill your order and have it shipped. On the other hand, if you say "Alexa, reorder toothbrushes," Alexa will search your order history for the last time you ordered that product, and place a new order for your previous purchase.

Whether playing with family, friends, or solo, add a new and unpredictable dimension to your Fortnite game with this clever Alexa skill. Receive a random drop location, or get a random challenge that you'll need to complete for the upcoming game.

ENHANCED EXPERIENCE WITH SCREENS

IN-SKILL PURCHASES AVAILABLE

GREAT FOR ALL AGES

ENABLE: *Alexa, enable Fortnite Challenges.*
THEN USE: *Alexa, open Fortnite Challenges.*
Alexa, ask Fortnite Challenges where I should land.

Interested in video games?
This flash briefing provides the latest news
and stories from the gaming industry
on a daily basis.

**#1 NEWS SKILL
IN THE US AND THE UK**

FLASH BRIEFING

ENABLE: *Alexa, enable Gaming Observer:
A Video Games News Flash Briefing.*
THEN USE: *Alexa, play my flash
briefing. Alexa, what's in the news?*

Control your Rachio smart sprinklers
from any Alexa-enabled
device using this Alexa skill.

REQUIRES ADDITIONAL
ACCOUNT AND HARDWARE

ENABLE: *Alexa, enable Rachio.*
THEN USE: *Alexa, open Rachio.*
Alexa, ask Rachio to stop watering.

Enjoy the Alexa version of the family-friendly game show by answering as many questions as you can, ranging from first grade to fifth grade in difficulty. Play in teams or solo.

**GREAT FOR
ALL AGES**

ENABLE: *Alexa, enable Are You Smarter Than A 5th Grader.*
THEN USE: *Alexa, play Are You Smarter Than A 5th Grader.*

This clever Alexa skill provides verbal motivation to writers to get back to the task at hand: writing! Alexa will talk to you as much or as little as you need to get back to work.

ENABLE: *Alexa, enable Writing Motivation.*
THEN USE: *Alexa, open Writing Motivation.*

Owners of Ford vehicles with electric batteries
can use this handy Alexa skill to lock
or unlock the car, to give the status of the
battery or vehicle itself, or to provide
information on the last trip the car took.

BEST ALEXA SKILLS
(PCMAG.COM)

REQUIRES ONLINE
ACCOUNT

ENABLE: *Alexa, enable MyFord Mobile.*
THEN USE: *Alexa, open MyFord Mobile.*

Play some light classical music
from Bach to help create a good environment
for studying or focusing on a specific task.

**GREAT FOR
ALL AGES**

ENABLE: *Alexa, enable Classical Study Music.*
THEN USE: *Alexa, open Classical Study Music.*

KNOW
THE CODE

Want to protect against unwanted purchases
made through your Alexa-enabled devices?
Go to your Alexa app, navigate to Settings, go to your
Alexa Account, go to Voice Purchasing, and enable
Voice Code to require a four-digit code anytime
someone tries to make a purchase.

Enjoy a fun, family-oriented approach to yoga.
More than 30 animal poses are included,
from armadillos and bats to kangaroos,
sharks, and wolves.

**BEST ALEXA SKILLS
(PCMAG.COM)**

**GREAT FOR
ALL AGES**

ENABLE: *Alexa, enable Animal Yoga.*
THEN USE: *Alexa, open Animal Yoga.*

You can receive a wide variety
of information on credit card, checking,
savings, and auto loan accounts
through Alexa and the Capital One skill.

**ALEXA BANKING
SKILL OF THE YEAR
(2019 ALEXA CONFERENCE)**

ENABLE: *Alexa, enable Capital One.*
THEN USE: *Alexa, ask Capital One how much did
I spend at Target last month? Alexa, ask Capital
One what's my payoff quote on my auto loan?
Alexa, ask Capital One to pay my credit card bill.*

Alexa meets Clue: St. Noire is a stylish murder-mystery board game (sold separately), which uses Alexa to interview suspects. St. Noire was created by legendary entrepreneur Nolan Bushnell and Hollywood visual design veteran Zai Ortiz.

PG
PARENTAL GUIDANCE
SUGGESTED

+
REQUIRES ACCOMPANYING
BOARD GAME

MURDER MYSTERY GAME

ENABLE: *Alexa, enable St. Noire.*
THEN USE: *Alexa, play St. Noire.*

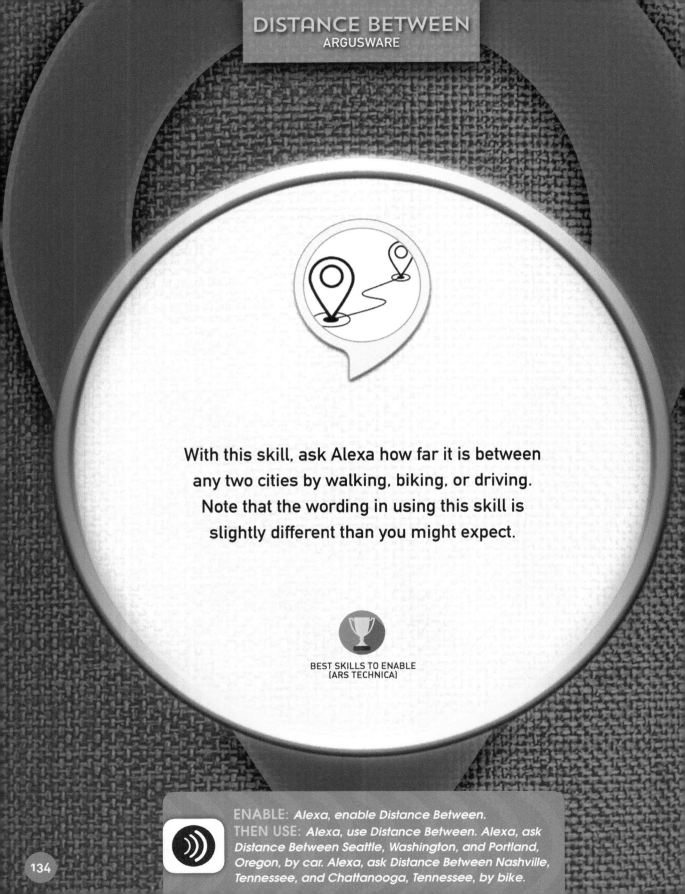

With this skill, ask Alexa how far it is between any two cities by walking, biking, or driving. Note that the wording in using this skill is slightly different than you might expect.

BEST SKILLS TO ENABLE
(ARS TECHNICA)

ENABLE: *Alexa, enable Distance Between.*
THEN USE: *Alexa, use Distance Between. Alexa, ask Distance Between Seattle, Washington, and Portland, Oregon, by car. Alexa, ask Distance Between Nashville, Tennessee, and Chattanooga, Tennessee, by bike.*

Compete to name the song title and artist
for a wide variety of songs spanning
five decades of popular music.
Compete with family and friends
or against strangers across the country.

THE BEST GAMES
TO PLAY WITH ALEXA
[DIGITAL TRENDS]

ENABLE: *Alexa, enable Song Quiz.*
THEN USE: *Alexa, play Song Quiz.*

All you have to do is say "Alexa, tell SafeTrek
to send help," and SafeTrek will have
one of their certified agents send help
to your home anytime, day or night.

**2019 ALEXA SKILL OF
THE YEAR - SMART HOME
(2019 ALEXA CONFERENCE)**

**REQUIRES ADDITIONAL
ACCOUNT**

ENABLE: *Alexa, enable SafeTrek.*
THEN USE: *Alexa, tell SafeTrek to
send help. Alexa, tell SafeTrek I'm hurt.*

Ask Alexa, using this Zoo Keeper skill,
to play the sound of any animal—great
for kids of all ages.

**GREAT FOR
ALL AGES**

ENABLE: *Alexa, enable Zoo Keeper.*
THEN USE: *Alexa, ask Zoo Keeper to play
the sound of a lion. Alexa, ask Zoo Keeper
what does the whale say?*

137

MANAGE YOUR
VOICE RECORDINGS

Amazon allows you to delete
your voice recordings at any time,
over any span of time. Go to the Alexa app,
navigate to Settings, navigate to Alexa Account,
and go to History. There, you can not only delete
your recordings, but you can also enable the ability to
delete voice recordings via voice command to Alexa.

Enjoy numerous audio clips, archival images, and more from the PBS documentary "America's Victoria: Remembering Victoria Woodhull." Designed for fans of American history and women's studies, this Alexa skill provides a dynamic education on an inspiring figure.

**ENHANCED EXPERIENCE
WITH SCREENS**

ENABLE: *Alexa, enable America's Victoria.*
THEN USE: *Alexa, open America's Victoria.*

Use any Alexa-enabled device to control your Xbox: Turn it on and off, start specific games, record videos, take screenshots, start party chats, and more.

REQUIRES ADDITIONAL
HARDWARE AND ACCOUNT

ENABLE: *Alexa, enable Xbox.*
THEN USE: *Alexa, turn on Xbox.*
Alexa, tell Xbox to launch The Division 2.

Big Sky provides "hyper-local" weather forecasts, tied to your actual street address. Premium features, unlockable through purchase, include radar imagery on Echo devices with screens, along with the ability to track multiple locations.

IN-SKILL PURCHASES AVAILABLE

ENHANCED EXPERIENCE WITH SCREENS

ENABLE: *Alexa, enable Big Sky.*
THEN USE: *Alexa, ask Big Sky if it will rain in two hours.*
Alexa, ask Big Sky if it will be sunny this afternoon.

This interactive story, set during the timeline of the movie *Jurassic World: Fallen Kingdom*, is an excellent audio-driven narrative on Alexa. Enjoy the first episode for free, with the option to purchase the remaining five separately.

PART OF THE 2018
MARKETING DIVE
CAMPAIGN OF THE YEAR

IN-SKILL PURCHASES
AVAILABLE

ENABLE: *Alexa, enable Jurassic World.*
THEN USE: *Alexa, play Jurassic World.*

Have young kids? Then Baby Groot
is for you. No matter what you ask Baby Groot,
the response is always the same:
"I am Groot." And it gets a lot of laughs
from the younger set.

ENABLE: *Alexa, enable Baby Groot.*
THEN USE: *Alexa, ask Baby Groot what day is it tomorrow. Alexa, ask Baby Groot how far away Mars is.*

Legendary publicity veteran Amy Summers shares one tip each day on how to improve getting your message across, using modern technology alongside classic techniques. Great for anyone in business or seeking to become a better communicator.

FLASH BRIEFING

ENABLE: *Alexa, enable The Pitch with Amy Summers.*
THEN USE: *Alexa, play my Flash Briefing.*
Alexa, what's in the news?

Lead a team of paranormal investigators as they hunt down ghosts. Voiced by Dan Aykroyd and Ernie Hudson, two of the original movie's cast members, this skill features high-end audio production throughout.

IN-SKILL PURCHASES
AVAILABLE

ENABLE: *Alexa, enable Ghostbusters.*
THEN USE: *Alexa, play Ghostbusters.*

DEAL OR
NO DEAL

Ask, "Alexa, what are your deals?"
And you'll receive a number of offers exclusive
to Prime members, including the price
and how much each item is discounted.

This Alexa skill provides educators
with a wide variety of brief guided activities
to supplement the day's curriculum
and refocus students as needed.

**REQUIRES ONLINE
ACCOUNT**

ENABLE: *Alexa, enable My Class.*
THEN USE: *Alexa, open My Class.*

Manage the Blackbears in this fun baseball simulation for Amazon Alexa. Play the free version from the 7th inning on, down 3-2, or unlock the full game to play a full nine innings.

IN-SKILL PURCHASES AVAILABLE

GREAT FOR ALL AGES

ENABLE: *Alexa, enable Seventh Inning Stretch.*
THEN USE: *Alexa, play Seventh Inning Stretch.*

Listen to more than 300 channels
of SiriusXM through any
Alexa-enabled device.

**PARENTAL GUIDANCE
SUGGESTED**

**REQUIRES ADDITIONAL
ACCOUNT**

ENABLE: *Alexa, enable SiriusXM.*
THEN USE: *Alexa, play SiriusXM.*
Alexa, play '80s on 8 on SiriusXM.

Enjoy an audio-only version of Bethesda's
award-winning Elder Scrolls V: Skyrim,
adapted in a text-based adventure style.

PG

PARENTAL GUIDANCE
SUGGESTED

ENABLE: *Alexa, enable Skyrim.*
THEN USE: *Alexa, play Skyrim.*

Control your Neptune Apex aquarium
through Alexa with this Alexa skill:
Receive status reports about water
temperature and composition,
feed your fish, and turn
outlets on and off.

ENABLE: *Alexa, enable Apex Fusion.*
THEN USE: *Alexa, open Apex Fusion.*
Alexa, ask Apex Fusion for a status report.

Have a conversation with Pikachu! Pikachu can tell you a story, use the Thunderbolt move, and even sing you "Happy Birthday." This skill is great for Pokemon lovers of all ages.

**25 AMAZING
KID- FRIENDLY ALEXA SKILLS
(TURBOFUTURE.COM)**

ENABLE: *Alexa, enable Pikachu Talk.*
THEN USE: *Alexa, open Pikachu Talk.*
Alexa, ask Pikachu to tell me a funny story.

Ask Alexa for daily bus arrival times
for your nearby or favorite stop,
across a variety of cities
in the United States and Canada.

ENABLE: *Alexa, enable OneBusAway.*
THEN USE: *Alexa, open OneBusAway.*

EVERYWHERE, THERE'S MUSIC

You can stream music throughout your home using your Echo devices. For Echo, Echo Dot, and Echo Show, you can play Amazon music accounts or third-party music services like Spotify, SiriusXM, TuneIn, Apple Music, and more. Create a group of Echo devices using the Alexa app, give that group a name, define your default music service within the Alexa app, rename devices to indicate location (also within the Alexa app), and then you can say "Alexa, play U2 downstairs" or "Alexa, play The Beatles on the outside speaker group."

Are you ready to have your mind read?
Think of a real or fictional character, and
Akinator will tell you which character you are
thinking about, after only a few questions.

BEST ALEXA SKILLS
(PCMAG.COM)

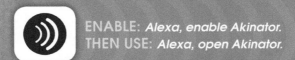

ENABLE: *Alexa, enable Akinator.*
THEN USE: *Alexa, open Akinator.*

Turn your jacuzzi on and off,
check the water temperature,
and more with this Alexa skill.

ENABLE: *Alexa, enable my hot tub.*
THEN USE: *Alexa, open my hot tub.*

Enjoy holiday music year-round
with Christmas Radio. Note that when
you activate the skill, there may be a brief
delay between the spoken introduction
and when the music starts playing.

GREAT FOR
ALL AGES

ENABLE: *Alexa, enable Christmas Radio.*
THEN USE: *Alexa, open Christmas Radio.*

Learn which movie and
game selections are available
at local Redbox kiosks, as well as more
information about specific releases.

ENABLE: *Alexa, enable Redbox.*
THEN USE: *Alexa, open Redbox.*
Alexa, ask Redbox what's new.

Use your voice to give simple voice commands and guide Batman through four compelling interactive experiences.

**GREAT FOR
ALL AGES**

ENABLE: *Alexa, enable Batman Adventures.*
THEN USE: *Alexa, play Batman Adventures.*

With this Alexa skill from HP, you can
ask your printer to print your shopping list,
a coloring page from Crayola or Just Add
Color, today's comics or crossword puzzle,
a calendar, and much more.

**REQUIRES ADDITIONAL
HARDWARE AND ACCOUNT**

ENABLE: *Alexa, enable HP Printer.*
THEN USE: *Alexa, ask My Printer to print
today's comics. Alexa, ask My Printer to
print my shopping list.*

Set within the universe of the Amazon Prime Video animated series *Kung Fu Panda: The Paws of Destiny*, Master Po will instruct his panda students in Kung Fu moves and knowledge in this kid-friendly interactive adventure.

3 ALEXA SKILLS YOU NEED TO KNOW RIGHT NOW (KIM KOMANDO)

GREAT FOR ALL AGES

ENABLE: *Alexa, enable Kung Fu Panda.*
THEN USE: *Alexa, play Kung Fu Panda.*

LIVING IN
THE BACKGROUND

You can change the wallpaper of any Amazon Echo device with a screen, such as the Echo Show or Echo Spot. Go to the Alexa app, go to the Devices tab, select your device from the list, navigate to Home Screen Background, and select your desired picture from your mobile device.

ANTHEM
ANTHEM INC

Anthem's Alexa skill answers
a variety of questions questions about both
health care and health insurance.

ENABLE: *Alexa, enable Anthem.*
THEN USE: *Alexa, open Anthem.*
Alexa, ask Anthem to define co-pay.

As the lord of the realm,
make choices—some easy,
some hard—and try to stay in power.

**THE BEST GAMES
TO PLAY WITH ALEXA
[DIGITAL TRENDS]**

**IN-SKILL PURCHASES
AVAILABLE**

ENABLE: *Alexa, enable Yes Sire.*
THEN USE: *Alexa, open Yes Sire.*

This Alexa skill plays music designed
to complement meditation, yoga,
or other relaxation-focused settings.

**GREAT FOR
ALL AGES**

 ENABLE: *Alexa, enable Healing Music.*
THEN USE: *Alexa, start Healing Music.*
Alexa, play Healing Music.

Created by a team of gaming industry
veterans, this highly rated interactive space
adventure makes you leader of a robot army
as you defeat the aliens, reclaim
your vessel, and survive the Vortex.

FEATURED ON AMAZON'S
ALEXA DEVELOPER BLOG

IN-SKILL PURCHASES
AVAILABLE

ENABLE: *Alexa, enable The Vortex.*
THEN USE: *Alexa, play The Vortex.*

Work out with a number of fun basketball-oriented drills brought to you by the WNBA's Seattle Storm and their superstar, Sue Bird. It's great for all ages and fitness levels.

**GREAT FOR
ALL AGES**

ENABLE: *Alexa, enable Storm Workout.*
THEN USE: *Alexa, open Storm Workout.*

Interact with a wide variety of Husqvarna lawnmowers with this Alexa skill: Start them, pause them, or have them run for a set period of time.

ADDITIONAL ACCOUNT REQUIRED

ENABLE: *Alexa, enable Automower.*
THEN USE: *Alexa, open Automower.*
Alexa, ask Automower to start.

Spend some time in this fun interactive space
adventure where timely decisions will keep
your ship supplied and your crew alive
across numerous in-game scenarios.
No two journeys are the same.

**8 BEST NEW ALEXA
SKILLS & UPDATES
(VOICEBREW)**

ENABLE: *Alexa, enable My Spaceship.*
THEN USE: *Alexa, start My Spaceship.*

ON YOUR GUARD

Alexa can guard your home by notifying you
if it hears any alarming noises like smoke alarms
or breaking glass. Go to the Alexa app, navigate
to Settings within the menu options, go to Guard,
and activate Alexa Guard. Then, all you have to do
is say "Alexa, I'm leaving," and Alexa Guard will
be activated. Upon your return, just say "Alexa,
I'm home," and Guard will deactivate.

Play any chapter from the Holy Quraan, create custom playlists of chapters, select translations in English or Urdu, choose between eight different reciters, and more.

2019 ALEXA CONFERENCE AWARD FINALIST

ENABLE: *Alexa, enable Holy Quraan.*
THEN USE: *Alexa, open Holy Quraan.*
Alexa, ask Holy Quraan to recite Chapter 48.

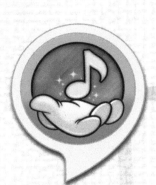

Test your knowledge of Disney songs!
Have fun with family or friends guessing titles,
characters, and lyrics from some of the most
popular tunes from your favorite films.

GREAT FOR
ALL AGES

ENABLE: *Alexa, enable Disney Hits Challenge.*
THEN USE: *Alexa, open Disney Hits Challenge.*

For all Chevrolet vehicles from model year 2011 until now, you can use this Alexa skill to interact with your car remotely. Start and stop the engine, lock and unlock the doors, and more.

REQUIRES ADDITIONAL ACCOUNT

ENABLE: *Alexa, enable myChevrolet.*
THEN USE: *Alexa, open Chevrolet.*
Alexa, ask Chevrolet to start my car.
Alexa, ask Chevrolet to lock all my cars.

If you like Netflix's show *3%*, you'll love this Alexa skill which features a variety of voice-based challenges and an interactive prequel story voiced by Bianca Comparato.

IN-SKILL PURCHASES
AVAILABLE

ENABLE: *Alexa, enable 3%.*
THEN USE: *Alexa, open 3%.*

Begin the process of applying for jobs at your local McDonald's restaurants with this handy Alexa skill. Answer a few questions, and Alexa will follow up with you via text message to continue the process.

ENABLE: *Alexa, enable McDonald's Apply Thru.*
THEN USE: *Alexa, open McDonald's Apply Thru.*

Keck
Medicine
of USC

This Alexa skill is for patients within
the Keck Medicine of USC system
and allows users to search for hospitals,
clinics, primary care physicians,
emergency rooms, and more.

TOP 7 HEALTH CARE
ALEXA SKILLS
(VOICEMARKETDATA)

REQUIRES ONLINE
ACCOUNT

ENABLE: *Alexa, enable Keck Medicine of USC.*
THEN USE: *Alexa, open USC Medicine.*

WHAT'S THE SCORE?

Get the latest updates on your favorite sports teams by simply asking, "Alexa, what's my sports update?" Go to the Alexa app, navigate to Settings from within the menu options, go to Sports, and select your favorite teams. From that point forward, asking Alexa for your sports update will produce up-to-the-minute news on your top teams.

Build a new order, place your Easy Order,
or order what you had most recently, all using
Domino's Pizza's Alexa skill. Once the order
is placed, simply ask Alexa about the
status of the order to receive real-time
updates along the way.

**THE BEST ALEXA SKILLS
(THE AMBIENT)**

**REQUIRES ADDITIONAL
ACCOUNT**

ENABLE: *Alexa, enable Domino's.*
THEN USE: *Alexa, open Domino's.*
Alexa, open Domino's and place an order.

Play with Elmo and learn the letter of the day, or play hide-and-seek, as part of Sesame Street's official Alexa skill.

2018 LIMA
LICENSING AWARD

180

ENABLE: *Alexa, enable Sesame Street.*
THEN USE: *Alexa, open Sesame Street.*
Alexa, ask Sesame Street to call Elmo.

KAYAK's Alexa skill lets you track flights and discover information about new destinations. To get the most out of it, you'll need to link to your KAYAK account, so you can book hotels via voice.

REQUIRES ADDITIONAL ACCOUNT

ENABLE: *Alexa, enable KAYAK.*
THEN USE: *Alexa, ask KAYAK how much it costs to fly from New York City to San Francisco. Alexa, ask KAYAK to book a hotel.*

Play a secret agent and craft your
own story in this immersive,
memorable interactive radio drama.

**IN-SKILL PURCHASES
AVAILABLE**

**REQUIRES ADDITIONAL
ACCOUNT**

**PARENTAL GUIDANCE
SUGGESTED**

ENABLE: *Alexa, enable Codename Cygnus.*
THEN USE: *Alexa, open Codename Cygnus.*

Nest

Use Alexa to control your Google Nest thermostat, any compatible smart-home devices, or in-home cameras with this handy Alexa skill.

ENHANCED EXPERIENCE WITH SCREENS

REQUIRES ADDITIONAL ACCOUNT

ENABLE: *Alexa, enable Google Nest.*
THEN USE: *Alexa, open Google Nest.*

Get relationship advice, play the Maury trivia game, preview upcoming episodes, and shop at the Maury store, all with this Alexa skill optimized for Echo devices with screens, like the Echo Show.

ENHANCED EXPERIENCE
WITH SCREENS

PG

PARENTAL GUIDANCE
SUGGESTED

ENABLE: *Alexa, enable Maury.*
THEN USE: *Alexa, open Maury.*

This skill is great for children learning elementary mathematics. Three difficulty levels—easy, medium, and hard—across addition, subtraction, multiplication, division, and more provide a fun challenge. Premium packs are available to purchase to add more questions and depth.

ONE OF THE BEST ALEXA SKILLS FOR KIDS (MASHABLE)

IN-SKILL PURCHASES AVAILABLE

ENABLE: *Alexa, enable 1-2-3 Math.*
THEN USE: *Alexa, open 1-2-3 Math.*

DEREGISTERING ALEXA DEVICES

If you want to sell or give away one of your Alexa-enabled devices, you can deregister the device from within your Alexa app. Open the app, navigate to Devices, click on the device you'd like to deregister, and click Deregister.

FITBIT
FITBIT, INC.

Track your daily progress with Alexa:
Ask Alexa if you hit your sleep goal, how you
did yesterday, or for your daily Fitbit stats.

BEST ALEXA SKILLS
(PCMAG.COM)

ENABLE: *Alexa, enable Fitbit.*
THEN USE: *Alexa, open Fitbit.*
Alexa, ask Fitbit how I'm doing today.

Stream any song or playlist
from Apple Music, as well as exclusive
interviews from Beats 1 Radio, via your
Alexa-enabled device by using
the Apple Music Alexa skill.

**REQUIRES ADDITIONAL
ACCOUNT**

ENABLE: *Alexa, enable Apple Music.*
THEN USE: *Alexa, open Apple Music.*
Alexa, play music by Snow Patrol on Apple Music.

Learn how to make the most
out of your personal or professional
Instagram account from this daily,
information-rich, three-minute flash briefing.

FLASH BRIEFING

ENABLE: *Alexa, enable The Instagram Stories.*
THEN USE: *Alexa, play my flash briefing.*

Find out easily and quickly whether an item is recyclable, based on a large knowledge database culled by the folks at Glad. Also included are a number of recycling tips to help educate you and your family.

BEST ALEXA SKILLS OF 2018
(BEST PRODUCTS)

ENABLE: *Alexa, enable Glad Recycler.*
THEN USE: *Alexa, talk to Glad Recycler.*
Alexa, ask Glad Recycler if I can recycle my pizza box.

Enjoy a wide variety of popular contemporary Christian artists, from Chris Tomlin to Lauren Daigle to Casting Crowns and more, with this Alexa skill. Select between K-LOVE Live (live radio), K-LOVE Classics (classic playlist), or K-LOVE Christmas (seasonal playlist).

ENABLE: *Alexa, enable K-LOVE.*
THEN USE: *Alexa, open K-LOVE.*

Listen to one of three shows provided by *The Washington Post*: "Post Reports," a news show; "The Daily 202's Big Idea," a political analysis show; or "Retropod," a daily show featuring one fascinating moment in history. You can also ask *The Washington Post* for the day's headlines.

ENABLE: *Alexa, enable The Washington Post.*
THEN USE: *Alexa, open The Washington Post.*
Alexa, ask The Washington Post for headlines.

Prepare for war against The Dark Citadel in this interactive role-playing experience. Use Echo devices with screens for a more immersive experience, and check your performance on the online leaderboard!

IN-SKILL PURCHASES AVAILABLE

ENHANCED EXPERIENCE WITH SCREENS

ENABLE: *Alexa, enable The Dark Citadel.*
THEN USE: *Alexa, play The Dark Citadel.*

ALEXA HAS
A HUNCH

Using deep neural networks to understand
human behavior, Alexa can detect if something
is different or amiss within your smart-home
configuration and proactively alert you, so you can
decide if there's a problem and act on it. Hunches
are on by default, but this setting can be
changed within the Alexa app by going to
the menu in the top left, selecting Settings,
and then deactivating Hunches.

This Alexa skill simulates owning
a lemonade stand and is a great way for older
children and adults to learn economic
concepts while having fun.

TOP ALEXA SKILL OF 2018
(DIGITAL TRENDS)

GREAT FOR
ALL AGES

ENABLE: *Alexa, enable Lemonade Stand.*
THEN USE: *Alexa, open Lemonade Stand.*

195

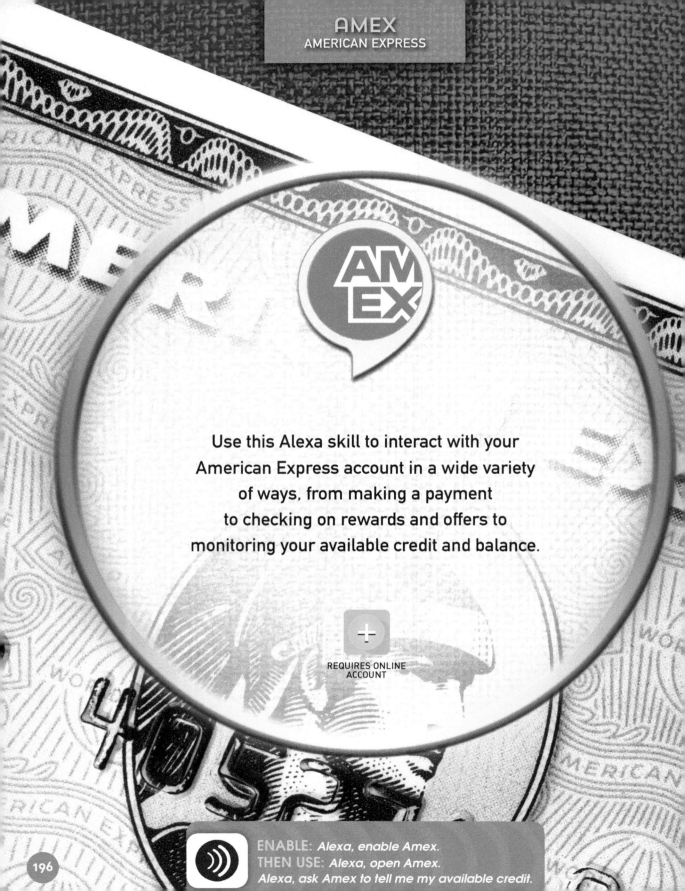

Use this Alexa skill to interact with your American Express account in a wide variety of ways, from making a payment to checking on rewards and offers to monitoring your available credit and balance.

REQUIRES ONLINE ACCOUNT

ENABLE: *Alexa, enable Amex.*
THEN USE: *Alexa, open Amex.*
Alexa, ask Amex to tell me my available credit.

Order any variety of Uber car by voice through Alexa. Set your Alexa location as your Uber default, inquire as to the location of your Uber ride, cancel your ride as necessary, and manage your Uber account all through this Alexa skill.

BEST ALEXA SKILLS
(PCMAG.COM)

REQUIRES ADDITIONAL
ACCOUNT

ENABLE: *Alexa, enable Uber.*
THEN USE: *Alexa, open Uber. Alexa, ask Uber to get me a ride to the airport.*

Book a reservation at one of thousands
of restaurants using OpenTable's Alexa skill.
Once booked, you'll receive an email that
you can then use to cancel or modify
the reservation if necessary.

BEST ALEXA SKILLS
(PCMAG.COM)

**REQUIRES ONLINE
ACCOUNT**

ENABLE: *Alexa, enable OpenTable.*
THEN USE: *Alexa, launch OpenTable.*

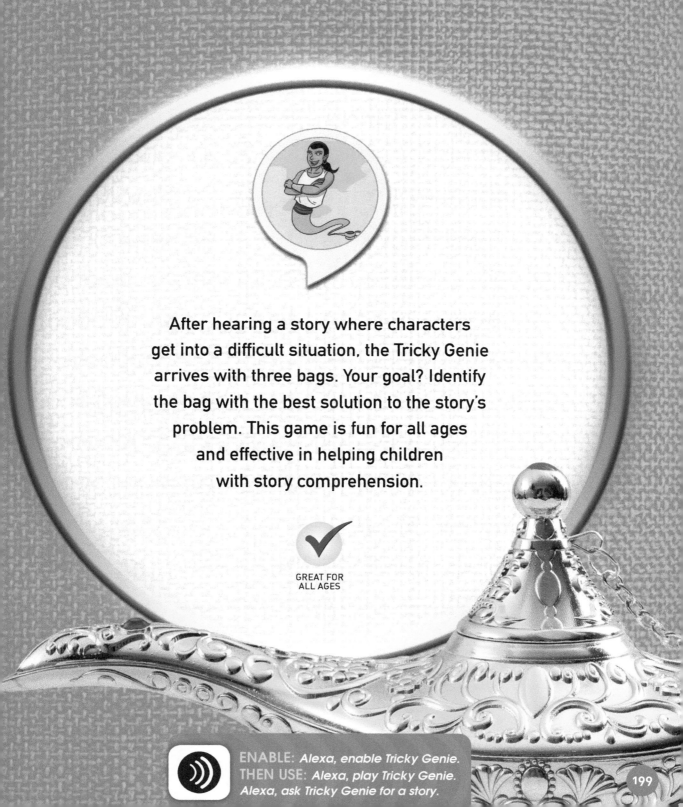

After hearing a story where characters get into a difficult situation, the Tricky Genie arrives with three bags. Your goal? Identify the bag with the best solution to the story's problem. This game is fun for all ages and effective in helping children with story comprehension.

GREAT FOR ALL AGES

ENABLE: *Alexa, enable Tricky Genie.*
THEN USE: *Alexa, play Tricky Genie.*
Alexa, ask Tricky Genie for a story.

Enjoy this calming Alexa skill, optimized for devices with screens such as the Echo Show and Echo Spot, that plays ocean waves in a perfect loop. With this skill, you can ask Alexa for the time, to run a timer, or any number of other basic functions, and the ocean waves will resume upon completing the request.

ENHANCED EXPERIENCE WITH SCREENS

ENABLE: *Alexa, enable Ambient Visuals: Ocean Waves.*
THEN USE: *Alexa, open Ocean Waves.*

Enjoy a fun, interactive kids' sing-along
to the classic childhood song
"The Muffin Man."

**ENHANCED EXPERIENCE
WITH SCREENS**

ENABLE: *Alexa, enable Muffin Man.*
THEN USE: *Alexa, open Muffin Man.*

amazon alexa
BUILT-IN FUNCTION

CHANGE THE
WAKE WORD

Alexa-enabled devices don't have to be
woken up with the word "Alexa." Amazon gives
you four choices: "Alexa," "Amazon," "Echo,"
and the *Star Trek*-like "Computer."

To make the change, go to the Alexa app,
select the Devices tab at the bottom, select
the device, and then select Wake Word.
If you change the wake word, the light indicator
on your device will briefly flash orange.

A growing number of localities have Alexa skills designed to make it easier to find recommended places to eat, play, and stay. Princeton Scoop is one such skill that will help you maximize your time while visiting Princeton, New Jersey.

ENHANCED EXPERIENCE
WITH SCREENS

ENABLE: *Alexa, enable Princeton Scoop.*
THEN USE: *Alexa, open Princeton Scoop. Alexa, ask Princeton Scoop to tell me a place to eat.*

This clever Alexa skill has children transform into different animals as they exercise, motivating them with positive encouragement along the way.

TOP ALEXA SKILL OF 2018 (DIGITAL TRENDS)

IN-SKILL PURCHASES AVAILABLE

ENHANCED EXPERIENCE WITH SCREENS

GREAT FOR ALL AGES

ENABLE: *Alexa, enable Animal Workout.*
THEN USE: *Alexa, open Animal Workout.*

With Ticketmaster's Alexa skill,
you can discover new events like concerts,
sporting events, and festivals, and use Alexa
to purchase verified tickets.

**REQUIRES ONLINE
ACCOUNT**

ENABLE: *Alexa, enable Ticketmaster.*
THEN USE: *Alexa, open Ticketmaster.*

Choose from one of six calming sounds, including a couple of different types of white noise, to soothe your baby and help her and you both get some much-needed sleep.

ENABLE: *Alexa, enable Baby Sleep White Noise.*
THEN USE: *Alexa, start Baby Sleep White Noise.*

Get the latest on politics, entertainment, sports and more from FOX by using this Alexa skill. Use the Alexa app to customize your flash briefing, so you can get the best of what you want.

FLASH BRIEFING

ENHANCED EXPERIENCE
WITH SCREENS

ENABLE: *Alexa, enable FOX News.*
THEN USE: *Alexa, open FOX News.*
Alexa, play my flash briefing.

207

MIXOLOGIST
LUIS SALA

Search a carefully curated collection of choice craft cocktails with this award-winning Alexa skill.

BEST ALEXA SKILLS (PCMAG.COM)

ENHANCED EXPERIENCE WITH SCREENS

PG PARENTAL GUIDANCE SUGGESTED

ENABLE: *Alexa, enable Mixologist.*
THEN USE: *Alexa, open Mixologist. Alexa, ask Mixologist what cocktails I can make with vodka. Alexa, ask Mixologist to surprise me.*

Does your Ford vehicle have SYNC Connect?
If so, you can use this Alexa skill to start
or stop the vehicle, lock or unlock the doors,
check tire pressure, and more.

REQUIRES ADDITIONAL
ACCOUNT

ENABLE: *Alexa, enable FordPass.*
THEN USE: *Alexa, open FordPass.*
Alexa, tell FordPass to start my car, using pin 1234.
Alexa, tell FordPass to lock my car.

Use this Alexa skill once a day to be guided
through one specific housecleaning task
with step-by-step, easy-to-follow instructions.
The skill includes a number of extra
time-saving tips, and has the ability
to send you an email with more
advice and special offers.

ENABLE: *Alexa, enable Clorox Clean.*
THEN USE: *Alexa, open Clorox Clean.*

Get scores, standings,
and real-time updates on your
favorite baseball teams.

IN-SKILL PURCHASES
AVAILABLE

 ENABLE: *Alexa, enable Baseball Live.*
THEN USE: *Alexa, open Baseball Live.*

THINGS TO TRY

Amazon has gone to great lengths to list Alexa's myriad types of features and functions—and you may not know about them all. To see the latest version of this list, go to the Alexa app, and within the menu options, select Things To Try.

ALEXA SKILL CATEGORIES

HEALTH & WELLNESS

KIDS

MUSIC

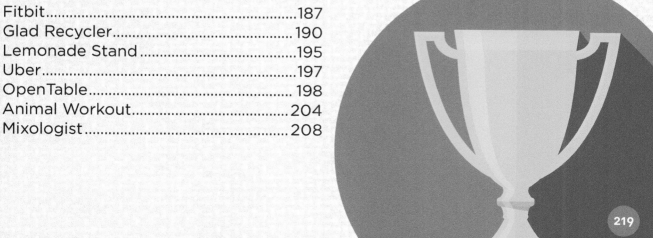

IN-SKILL PURCHASES

REQUIRES ADDITIONAL ACCOUNT

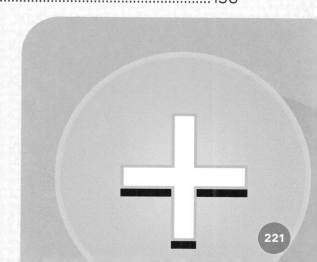

REQUIRES ADDITIONAL ACCOUNT

ENHANCED EXPERIENCE WITH SCREENS

FLASH BRIEFINGS

PARENTAL GUIDANCE

CPSIA information can be obtained
at www.ICGtesting.com
Printed in the USA
BVHW020401151119
563901BV00001B/1/P

9 780991 141890